Congratulations on taking a major step forward toward creating more personal and financial freedom for yourself!

Get all of the bonus material mentioned in this book at
www.happycustomerformula.com/bestintown

BEST *in* TOWN

How To Create Five Star Reviews and
Massive Profits in Your Restaurant

MARK BARES

Copyright © 2018 Mark Bares.

Contact Mark Bares at
phone: (715) 409-6794
email: hello@happycustomerformula.com
get all of the bonus material mentioned in this book at
www.happycustomerformula.com/bestintown

All rights reserved. No part of this book may be reproduced, stored, or transmitted by any means—whether auditory, graphic, mechanical, or electronic—without written permission of both publisher and author, except in the case of brief excerpts used in critical articles and reviews. Unauthorized reproduction of any part of this work is illegal and is punishable by law.

CONTENTS

Introduction vii
Chapter 1   What is Success? 1
Chapter 2   My Story 5
Chapter 3   The Only Show in Town 11
Chapter 4   A Battle Of Biblical Proportions 15
Chapter 5   Creating Culture 19
Chapter 6   Exceptional Expectations 27
Chapter 7   Creating Credibility 33
Chapter 8   Get in the Cloning Business 37
Chapter 9   Raise Your Standards 39
Chapter 10 Avoiding Hostage Situations 49
Chapter 11 Consistency is King 51
Chapter 12 Exceptional Productivity 53
Chapter 13 Missed Memories, New Opportunities 57
Chapter 14 Exceptional Success 59

INTRODUCTION

It's Survival of the Fittest...

Great customer service is no longer an option for restaurants, it's a matter of survival. If you own or manage a restaurant and one of the following describes you, this book is for you:

- I need major help. I spend a lot of my time fixing problems my employees create. I don't even remember what it was like to have a life outside of my business.
- My business is doing well, but I know we could do a lot better if I could just get my staff to all work together more.
- My business is great, but I'm always looking to create even better experiences for my guests.

The fact that you're even reading this book sets you apart from most of your competition. Most people keep on doing what they've always done and blame others for their lack of success. It's people just like you who know success lies squarely on your shoulders and the only way to truly get ahead is by taking action.

This book will give you tons of successful customer service strategies you can implement right now to create five star quality service getting your guests coming back more often and spending more money than ever before.

The one thing you need to keep in the back of your mind while reading this book is that you will never be able to cash in on the huge profit potential locked away inside your staff if you don't teach them how to implement the strategies on the following pages. Systematically training your staff on a continual basis is the key to both your personal and financial freedom.

> Do what you do so well they'll want to experience it again and bring their friends.
>
> —Walt Disney

> If you can't describe what you are doing as a process, you don't know what you're doing.
>
> —W. Edwards Deming

> Customers may forget what they ate or drank, but they'll never forget how you made them feel.
>
> —Mark Bares

Chapter 1

WHAT IS SUCCESS?

How do you measure success? The answer depends on who you ask. Some people measure success by the amount of cash in the register, the size of their bank account, or being able to walk away for a week with the comfort of knowing the business will run smoothly and keep making money without them there. Others consider a day successful if they are simply able to pay their bills and keep the lights on. Although those things are important, I believe true success happens when your customers leave a little happier than when they come in. Do that, and all other forms of success will follow.

Creating this kind of success is not easy. Did you know 60% of businesses fail before even making it through their first year and a whopping 80% go under before completing their fifth year of business? Unfortunately, the numbers aren't much better for restaurants.

"I want you to go out there and deliver great customer service!" has become a battle cry of many of these floundering businesses teetering on the brink of bankruptcy. The mantra of providing great customer service can be heard shouting from the rooftops of almost every business. Unfortunately, simply telling your staff to do it will not make it happen.

Customer service is not a product you can pull off a shelf. You won't find it on Amazon with two-day super saver shipping. And, unfortunately, there is no one single thing you can do to provide it for your guests.

There's a small pizza shop near my house that my family likes to go to regularly. The pizza is fantastic. Hands down, the best I've ever had. The first time we went there, we were greeted by a super friendly young lady named Sarah who ended up being our server. Sarah asked where we were from and throughout the evening I learned Sarah was saving up to go to college in Madison during the fall season and was hoping to make the volleyball team. Not only was the food delicious, but the service was fantastic. I think Sarah had a sixth sense because she always knew when I needed another pint of beer. We had a great time, and before we left, we were already planning when we could make it back out to the same pizzeria again.

We were able to make it back a couple of weeks later. Sarah wasn't working that night. Our new server's name was Scott. The only reason I know this is because I had to ask him. Scott was the complete opposite of Sarah. It took us forever to get our drinks. When we finally gave him our order, he screwed it up just about every way possible. And I didn't have to worry about driving home that night because one beer was all I was able to finagle out of Scott.

So why were our two experiences so different? How can you be guaranteed your guests won't suffer the same fate as we did? Great customer service isn't just an idea or a concept. It needs to be a concrete system your staff is consistently trained on.

WHAT IS SUCCESS?

I want you to think about the experiences you've had over the last couple of months. I'd be willing to bet you could name at least a dozen similar experiences. Up until three years ago, those were the same, erratic experiences my guests would have to endure. Until you construct your system of creating consistently outstanding customer experiences in your own business, that's probably what your guests are experiencing too.

Monthly staff meetings, bribes, threats, begging – nothing could tame the wild beast named Customer Service. The experiences my guests had changed from week to week, day to day, even hour to hour. The only way I could get my staff to come close to the mark was by planting myself in the middle of them. As soon as I walked away to take care of something, things seemed to go haywire.

Everything changed the day I created CREST. CREST stands for Creating Renowned Experiences thru Systemized Training. But CREST is more than just an acronym – it's an idea that can give you both more personal and financial freedom. CREST can become the greatest asset in your business, but it won't happen on it's own. It will be up to you to take what you learn in this book and implement CREST to create your own company culture, expectations, and training systems. If you do, I guarentee you'll be generating more five star reviews and massive profits than you ever have before!

CREST didn't come to me all at once. It's the culmination of years of study, going to conferences and seminars, and a lot of hard work. I started studying some of the most successful businesses from the past 80 years in America. I saw common threads that tied them all together. I realized the ideas implemented by these great companies could be tweaked to work in the hospitality industry to create incredible experiences and massive profits.

What I'm about to teach you has not only transformed my business, but it has changed my life. I owe CREST more than I could ever express. CREST gives me the freedom to come and go at work as I please. CREST has given my family the financial security to allow my wife, Laura, to stay home with our eight kids and even teach them at home! CREST is a money maker, and in the following pages, I'd love for you to get to know how CREST works so you can experience all the success I have.

Do you want more time with your family and friends? More time for yourself doing the fun stuff you always talked about, but could never find the time to do? Do you want to grow your business bigger than you could ever imagine and make more money? Do you want people in your town or city to refer to you and your business when they talk about the best restaurant or bar in town?

If you do, you need to get to know CREST well and fast.

Chapter 2

MY STORY

I know you're probably dying to get to know CREST. But first, I'm going to tell you a little about me.

My dad and grandpa moved to Merrill, Wisconsin in 1969 and purchased a local bowling alley. The years were good to them, and over time they added a large bar, restaurant, and a banquet facility.

I grew up in the family business and always loved working with dad and grandpa making people happy. After going to college for engineering, my dad asked if I would come back and work with him for a while. In college, I fell in love with calculus (I know I'm a nerd), but the idea of hanging out with friends working in the business with my family sounded way better than moving to some far-away big city spending long, boring hours in an office cubicle.

Times were good, and we coasted along. Back then making money was simple. All we had to do was open the doors and the cash came flowing in. We never had discussions about product development or our guest's experience. Food was food, beer was beer, and bowling was bowling; and employees were and an incidental tool to deliver each of those products. In fact, a lot of business owners of that time seemed to have the opinion that they were doing their customers a favor, not the other way around.

Then came the Great Recession of 2008. The housing bubble had finally burst, and everyone stopped spending money. The market, especially for the hospitality industry, became much more competitive. Consumers were holding on to their extra cash and every restaurant, tavern, movie theater, and bowling alley engaged in a no holds barred war to get them to spend those precious extra dollars with them.

Businesses who made the dreadfully terrible decision to compete on price were initially successful, but in the end, wound up in the waste bin of failed businesses. I knew lowering prices wasn't the answer, but I was also faced with the pressures of providing for a growing family and shrinking demographics in my area.

The competition was fierce and times got tough. My wife and I just had our fifth child, and as our family was growing, our town began to shrink. Our town is a blue-collar town and had lost 15% of its population over the course of about five years. Over a ten-year period, our school district had lost 25% of its student population.

As our town shrunk, so did our revenue. Deciding which bills would get paid was a weekly game I hated. My focus turned to cutting business costs, but deep down I knew it was a temporary solution and a losing battle. There are only two ways to make more money: cutting costs or growing revenue. Cutting costs will work for a while, but you can't cut so far before you cut your throat. Growing revenue was my only way out, but faced with a shrinking population and guests with less expendable income, I didn't know what to do.

MY STORY

I came to a crossroad; get a corporate job and work in a sterile office or do the seemingly impossible and figure out a way to grow revenue in such a dire economic situation. I chose the latter and started to read book after book on marketing.

My shift in strategy worked, for a while. More people were coming in the door every day, and business slowly started to grow, but something still wasn't quite right.

What I didn't realize was that customers' expectations had shifted over the years. Simply opening your doors for business was no longer enough. Today's guests expect so much more from their experiences than they ever have before. My marketing efforts were working great. We had tons of new faces coming through the door every day, but I began to notice those new customers were not returning as frequently as I had expected.

My wife wasn't too happy either. I was constantly getting called away from home to take care of problems my managers should have dealt with. Unhappy guests, arguments between employees, problems with vendors – all small stuff that I don't need to deal with.

The tipping point came on a cold February morning in 2013. That weekend we had a family reunion booked. They come every year to bowl, drink and have dinner. It was a rather large group that we could count on coming in year after year. I'm sure you have those kinds of annual groups in your business too. It's income we all sometimes take for granted.

Back then I worked most weekends, but on that particular Saturday, my wife was out of town, so I had to stay home with the kids (by that time we had six little ones at home). The Tuesday after the event, not only did I get a call from one of the party organizers about the poor service they received, I also got an angry letter from another participant of that group. Long story short, due to a scheduling mix-up by an employee, their party started quite a bit later than it should have. On top of that, my staff was not only indifferent to the fact that they were upset but responded to their complaints with veiled hostility.

I thank God every day for that disgruntled phone call and angry letter on that fateful day as it forced me to make a decision: fight or flight. I just couldn't walk away from our family business, and I still dreaded the idea of becoming a working stiff crammed away in an office cubicle for 8 to 12 hours a day.

So I fought back the only way I knew how – with books. I began reading every customer service book I could get my hands on. It was at this point that I realized I had too many books and not enough time, so I taught myself to speed-read and then I read even more books. I filled notebook upon notebook with notes on everything I read, and within about three months' time, CREST began to take shape.

The transformation in my business has been nothing short of miraculous. It didn't happen overnight, but we started transforming our occasional guests into regulars. And our regulars started spending more money. They began bringing friends and family with them, and we were able to convert them into regulars too.

Since competing on price alone is a battle I knew I would ultimately lose, I took a chance and raised my prices. My town filled with mostly blue-collar folks who work hard for every dollar they earn and can be penny pinchers interestingly barely batted an eye. I started to reinvest in my building heavily, and my staff and revenues began to soar. I grew gross revenues from $754,000 in 2014 to $849,000 in 2015. That's a 13% increase in just 12 months without spending an extra penny on marketing. In 2016 we grossed $904,000 and by the end of 2017 broke through $1,000,000. Not bad for a restaurant & bowling alley in a town of less than 9,000 in the Northwoods of Wisconsin!

But what I'm thankful for is the transformation that took place in my personal life. My wonderful wife, Laura, now stays home to raise our eight children. We homeschool our kids, and I'm able to stay home in the morning to teach them each math, science, and religion. I head into work around 9, or 10 am and am usually home in time for dinner. I can even take my family on vacation or just leave for a couple of days knowing that my business is not only making me money but making happy guests who will come back again and again while I'm away.

CREST has transformed my business and my life. I think it's about time you discover CREST for yourself.

Chapter 3

THE ONLY SHOW IN TOWN

In developing CREST, the first thing I did was define my competition. Knowing who and what your competing against will help you get a good sense of how and why your potential customers make their buying decisions. Even if you're in a small town, competition is a lot more fierce than you might have thought.

So grab a piece of paper and a pen because we're going to do a little homework. Turn the paper 90 degrees and make three columns. Now it's time to do some thinking…

In the first column, write down all the businesses that you are in direct competition with. If you are a steakhouse, write down businesses that serve similar clientele within a five-mile radius. If you run a pizzaria, list other pizzarias. If you're a steak house, write down other local steak houses. If you own a sports bar, list the other sports bars in your area.

If this were the only competition you had to worry about, life would be pretty easy. In all honesty, most business's customer service sucks. Especially at a local level, most independently owned businesses are run by owners who are too busy working in their business. They are busy working the floor, fixing the plumbing, placing orders with vendors, and cooking in the kitchen to have time to train their staff properly to provide exemplary customer service. If this was truly your only competition, **all you would have to do is suck a little less than everyone else.**

That would be the life. Success would be as simple as visiting every place on that short list, take some notes on their service and systems, and tweak what you do to just suck a little less. You would be a customer service superstar compared to them!

Unfortunately, it's not that simple. Let's go back to our worksheet and fill in column number 2.

In this column, write down other local businesses within that same five-mile radius that are in the hospitality industry. This would include all restaurants, taverns, bowling alleys, movie theaters, family entertainment centers, roller skating rinks, and any other local business that competes for your prospective guests' time and money.

This list will take you a little longer to complete. Because of the larger list, your competition becomes a little more competitive. Sucking a little less than the competition becomes a little harder at this point, especially if there are any franchises on the list. Inevitably there will be at least a couple of locally owned business who are doing a few things right. It's going to take a little more work to raise your bar above theirs.

And competing with franchises can be even more difficult. They have entire departments at their national headquarters dedicated to improving their customer service delivery systems and training their local unit managers on how to train their staff with complete scripts, videos, handouts, and visual templates. There's a reason some of these franchises are as successful as they are and a huge part of their success is the corporate customer service training muscle they deliver. If you've ever researched franchises, you know that the franchisees pay a hefty price for that customer service success.

At this point, you've got a little more work to do in the customer service department. Things get a bit complicated. You'll need to start creating your unique company culture, define your guest's expectations, create a system to deliver consistent training to all staff members, and make sure you keep your sanity by creating an environment where your expectations are fulfilled without you being in your business 24 hours a day, seven days a week.

But we're not done with your homework yet! The last column is the one that should scare you the most, but also the one that will give you the biggest opportunity for growth once you realize its weakness.

In the last column, write down all the entertainment options your prospective guests have that do not require them to leave their house. Some examples are television, streamed movies and TV shows, surfing the internet, YouTube, picking up a six-pack of beer from the gas station, and ordering a pizza for delivery from the local pizzeria just to name a few.

All of those food, beverage, and entertainment options don't even require your prospective customer to leave their house! And people are inherently lazy – double whammy! Your staff needs to be so good at what they do that your guests are willing to put on a pair of pants (because they're probably sitting around in their underwear, right?), comb their hair, get in their car (in my case often in the middle of one of Wisconsin's famous 15 below zero freeze your ass off winter), drive through traffic which they have no patience for, to be served by your staff.

Are you providing a level of legendary customer service to motivate someone to do all of that?

The good news is that people are starting to revolt against the virtual, digital life the media is trying to push on us. In his book, *The Revenge Of Analogue: Real Things And Why They Matter*, author David Sax argues that people have been living too much in the digital realm. We are physical beings who deep down require physical relationships with real people and things. People are starting to come out of their cyber hibernation and their hunger for real social experiences with real people has been awakened.

What does a restaurant produce? How about a bar? Or a movie theater or a bowling alley? If all you are providing is a hamburger, a martini, a movie, or a game of bowling, you will end up losing to your competition. Remember, your competition isn't exactly what you thought it was. Take another look at the list you just made.

You need to provide a lot more if you want to truly succeed rather than simply stay in business. Five star service requires you to provide consistently extraordinary experiences that will make your guests come back more often ready to spend more money without even thinking about it. You need to become their go-to place for whatever it is you provide; not because you are the cheapest in town, but because you are the best. Period.

Chapter 4

A BATTLE OF BIBLICAL PROPORTIONS

We're going to go biblical here for a moment. Do you remember the story of David versus Goliath? My kids love it when I read them this story. It's a story that resonates with most people – deep down we want to be the little guy who courageously takes down the big, bad bully.

So how many people do you know who would say that Goliath is the good guy in that story? Yup – zero. The reason we all like this story so much is that everybody loves an underdog. The scrawny kid who's sick and tired of getting pushed around, so he stands up for himself and ends up victorious. There's a reason for this – most people see themselves as the underdog in their own lives. They go to work only to make money for someone else that doesn't appreciate them. Then they get to go home to family who takes them for granted and hang out with friends that take advantage of them. Rarely do they get any recognition for everything they do for everyone else.

People love it when someone sticks it to "The Man." Corporate America is always portrayed as the bad guy. The headlines usually read something like, "Corporate Fat Cats Getting Rich Of The

Sweat And Blood Of Average America." And this is where you have a prime opportunity to create fiercely loyal customers out of average Americans.

Many small, independently owned businesses incorrectly believe they don't stand a chance against the likes of the big chains and franchises. After all, how can you compete with a Goliath machine that is backed by not only millions of dollars, but also by incredibly brilliant and talented people who work at their corporate headquarters building their brand, creating new products, and implementing top-notch training procedures?

The truth is, deep down people recognize that the major chains and franchises are part of Corporate America. Try as they might, franchises can't hide the fact that they are essentially run by big, faceless corporate entities whose primary goal is profit at all costs.

And the bottom line is people don't like buying from big corporations or franchises; they like buying from people. The secret is delivering more than just the product you serve. Making a personal connection with your customers is key. Tell them about who you are and where you came from. Everyone has a story, and people love getting a glimpse into other people's lives. Reality TV has built an empire on this principle.

I am the third generation in my family to run our business. My father, Jim, and grandpa, Les, came to town in 1969 and bought the local bowling alley that had gone bankrupt two times since the place was built in 1962. The informal name of our business is ***Les & Jim's***. I not only include that name in all of our marketing, but I include a backstory to get people to buy into who and what we are. It's on the back of our menu. It's on our Yelp page. I even have an eight-foot by four-foot vintage picture of my dad and grandpa on the wall in the bowling alley. Why? So, people can learn about the history of my business. And when they learn about my history, they want to tell me their story. When that happens, we form a connection that goes beyond business and customer. In a way, we become extended family with each other.

Picture of Les and Jim – my dad and grandpa who bought the business in 1969.

I even take it a step further and teach my staff to get to know our customers. This is where CREST comes into play. I've made it a part of our customer service training system; we practice asking customer oriented open-ended questions, so my staff can find out more about the people they are serving. And in doing this, our guests form a bond not only with the staff member they are talking to but a bond with our local, hometown business. I look through the local paper each week and cut out articles that feature the accomplishments of residents. I'll mail them a card with a quick note and the cutout article from the paper. Can you name one franchise or corporation that does that?

The back cover of our menu – includes
a brief history of the business.

The fact that you are smaller than the big guy and don't have a big corporate office in Manhattan, but live, work, and shop in your community gives you an advantage the big guys will never have. Capitalize on it! Tell your staff what your story is. Teach them to share your story with your guests. Encourage your staff to find out what your guests' stories are. Invite your guests to become part of your extended family and price essentially becomes irrelevant.

You are David. Let's get ready to take down Goliath!

Chapter 5

CREATING CULTURE

Lately, there has been a lot of talk about company culture. Open any issue of the major business magazines like *Success* or *Entrepreneur* you'll find lots of articles dedicated to the subject. It has become a "buzz word" that very few people take the time to define, much less implement it in their own business. Much like the term "customer service," people spend a lot of time talking about it without giving normal people like you and me a concrete idea of what it is or how to implement it. To avoid having to go through the effort of helping you create your own company culture, they make it into something that is completely abstract. The use of vague terms like "values," "beliefs," and "attitudes" abound without giving you a system to help you or your employees form those beliefs, values, and attitudes.

In the hospitality business, many, if not most or all, employees show up for work for their shifts with the singular intention of getting a paycheck at the end of the week. People who work solely for a paycheck will do just enough to not lose that paycheck. No doubt you've spent a significant amount of time and money with the singular purpose of getting customers in the door hoping they'll continue to come back on a regular basis. The disconnect between what you're trying to accomplish and what your staff is trying to accomplish is costing you tons of money. Unfortunately, creating happy customers who come back time and again to spend their hard earned cash in your business is not on your employees' to-do list. Even if you tell them to create happy customers, their investment in your business usually doesn't go beyond doing the absolute bare minimum.

That's not to say your staff doesn't care about your business. Your continued success is required for them to get a paycheck and at the very minimum, most of your employees know this. You might even have some employees who go the extra mile to make your business a success. These employees are rare gifts. They are usually either a family friend, a valuable customer who decided to come on board and work for you (side note: these are some of our best employees!) or an aficionado of your niche.

So let's take the best-case scenario. Let's assume you have a full staff from the front of the house to the back of the house who are all close relatives and have a small financial stake in your restaurant. They want to see your business succeed because when it does, they make more money.

On Monday morning, you have a staff meeting with all of your best, most heavily invested employees to talk about customer service. You tell them that they all need to provide the very best in customer service so your guests will come back more often and spend more money than ever.

The problem is that everyone has a different idea of why they are there. In the case of a restaurant, the hostess will think it's her job to simply welcome guests and seat them. The wait staff believes it's their job to take orders, deliver drinks and food, and give the guests their bill. And your cook or chef will tell you they are there to cook the guests food. Well, I think you get the idea.

CREATING CULTURE

Company culture is essentially what your employee's beliefs, values, and attitudes toward their job and your company are. That's an easy enough concept, but forming your employee's beliefs, values, and attitudes into what you want them to be is the real trick. Lucky you, CREST has all the tools you need to make this happen in your business.

One of the first questions I was faced when I discovered the secret of CREST was "what business are you in?" My initial response was that I was in the restaurant business, tavern business, bowling business, kids birthday party business, and wedding reception business. After all, that's what all my ads and marketing said. And I thought that was what my customers were coming in to buy.

When I realized people don't even need to leave their living rooms to get core products I was delivering, I wrote this question on a piece of paper, "*why* do people buy all that stuff from *me*?" I stared at that piece of paper for a good long time slowly realizing that people don't come to my business to simply get a hamburger, a drink, or a game of bowling, no matter how good they are. People come to your business because they are looking for happiness. It is such a small, simple word, but it means the difference between incredible success and dismal failure.

Nine little letters perfectly and completely describe why your guests willingly hand over their hard earned money to you. It's why they walk through your door and not your competitor's door. It's also the reason they might never come back. There is so much sorrow, pain, and sadness around us every day. Whether they are going out for dinner, to a movie with friends, or taking their kids out for a round of mini golf, people are starving for happiness.

Take a moment to think about what motivates you. Two primary motivating factors make people do things. The first is to avoid pain and the second is to find pleasure. You can go all the way back to the very first man and woman. I guarantee you that one of these two motivating factors determined every decision they made.

Why was the first wheel invented? To avoid the pain of dragging heavy stuff around on someone's back. Why did I get a painful root canal done a couple of months ago? To avoid the bigger pain of sore tooth. Why do I buy my wife expensive earrings for our anniversary? Seeing her huge smile when she opens the package makes me very happy (and I avoid the pain of getting yelled at for forgetting our anniversary!) Think about all the decisions you make throughout your day today. I guarantee you they all come back to these two same motivating factors.

That's one of the neat things about being in the hospitality business. We get to bring joy and happiness to people who need it. But what does this have to do with company culture?

You need to get your staff not only to understand, but to truly believe that their real job is creating happiness for your guests. Whatever it is that they are physically doing, whether it's making drinks, taking orders, or mopping floors, is just the thing they happen to be doing which allows them to affect your guests' experience. Everything they do can bring your guests happiness. Sometimes it's simply contentment and other times it might be intense joy. Either way, happiness is the goal.

CREATING CULTURE

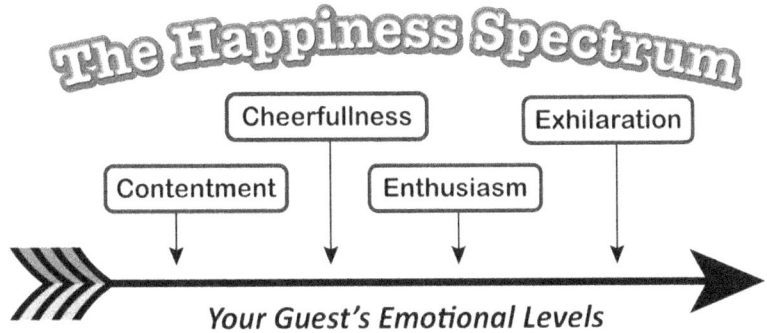

Your Guest's Emotional Levels

If you've ever been to Disney World, you know the incredible level of customer service they deliver. Disney is the undisputed king of customer service. I've spent considerable time studying Disney customer service and the systems they employ to deliver magical experiences for their guests. In his book, *"Be Our Guest: Perfecting the Art of Customer Service"* Theodore Kinni describes how Walt Disney delivers happiness to their guests. Disney has created an ingenious idea they call their Common Purpose.

Their Common Purpose is the reason they open their doors every day. It's the reason they spend so much time and money training their staff. It's the reason they go so far above and beyond to make their guests happy. It's the reason they can charge insane prices and still have guests coming back year after year after year.

Reading about Disney got me thinking that I need to be in the same business as Disney. I'm not talking about opening a theme park; I'm talking about delivering happiness. I realized that my common purpose was to "Create Happiness and Lasting Friendships for People of All Ages."

Now your Common Purpose might be a little different than mine. If you own a bar, you might not be creating happiness for people of ALL ages, but you should define exactly who you are serving. Define your best customer and put them in your common purpose. You might also change it to define how you create happiness more precisely. In my case, we provide so many different core products I decided to keep my customer purpose a bit more vague, but it still conveys the idea that we are so much more than a restaurant, bar, or bowling alley.

How do you get your staff to not only understand your common purpose, but more importantly to embrace it and live it in their jobs? They need to realize that your guests can get dinner delivered to them at home. It's easier to pick up a case of beer from the gas station than it is to come into your establishment. And just about everyone has all the entertainment they could ask for either hanging on their wall, or in their pocket on their phone.

People come to your business to find a bit of sunshine in an otherwise very dark world. That doesn't happen by simply giving them a plate of spaghetti or a vodka cranberry, but through the interactions they have with the staff. Your employees need to understand they play a vital role in the success of your business and that you are happy to pay them week after week because they honestly and truly are the only people who can bring every one of your guests happiness. And in doing that, your guest will happily come back time and time again.

In reality, your are actually selling an experience; an experience that brings happiness. I know it sounds like I'm beating a dead horse here, but it is an absolute necessity for real growth. The success or failure of your business depends on creating exceptional guest experiences on a consistent basis, and that will only happen if you consistently train your staff how to create those experiences. And when they start realizing the truth of these ideas, they will start taking ownership and pride in creating happiness for others. It's sort of like rolling a snowball down a hill. It takes a lot of work getting it started, but once it starts rolling, look out!

A side benefit of creating the right kind of company culture is that hiring becomes way easier because you'll start to attract better candidates for your positions. People may not directly recognize it, but on a subconscious level, they will start to recognize that your business is different. Positive, productive people are naturally drawn to organizations that have the right kind of company culture. You'll find you will no longer have to settle for a "warm body" in a position because you have no other choice. In fact, people will seek you out. You'll be able to sift the wheat from the chaff and pick the best person for each of your positions. In fact, I haven't paid for a "help wanted" ad in years. I do have some systems in place to attract job applicants, but I use them mainly to reel in the winners who are seeking me out.

One of the best benefits of creating a healthy, positive, well-defined company culture is that you won't have to work as hard to keep your staff motivated and on track. Once they understand why they are doing what they are doing, they "own" the ideas of creating happiness for your guests. When that happens, it's almost as if they are part owner of your company. That's because your company is no longer about making money for the boss, its real purpose is creating experiences that bring their guests (the guests are no longer your guests, they belong to your employees) happiness.

Instead of playing big brother who's always looking over everyone's shoulder making sure they are doing what you want them to do, you can relax knowing that your employees are looking out for your best interests. Why? Because they now know that your guest's happiness is everyone's primary interest. This even happens when you are not at work.

I made the change from being on the floor with my staff during almost all open hours to working a 9 am to 5 pm schedule a couple of years ago. That's not the normal schedule for someone who owns a restaurant. Most restaurateurs basically live in their centers. I still pop in to shake hands with my guests and make sure everything is running smoothly, but I've found that the more time I spend in my office, the more money I make.

Why? The answer is two-fold. First, I can focus more of my time on marketing and staff development. Second, when I leave my staff, they understand that I trust them to achieve our common purpose every night fully. They know that the time we spend in training and developing staff has given them the tools and skills they need to create happiness for everyone who walks in the door.

And they know that repeat visits, higher check totals, and happier customers mean more hours and more tips for them. And I know that all of that means more freedom and bigger profits for my family and me.

Chapter 6

EXCEPTIONAL EXPECTATIONS

Football in Wisconsin is a big thing and my second oldest son *loves* watching football. Believe it or not, he's the only one out of my eight kids who likes football. Every Sunday, he has his butt firmly anchored to the couch watching all of his favorite teams. Oddly enough, we live in Wisconsin, and he doesn't even like the Packers; his favorite team is the Falcons.

I've never been much of a football fan myself. From the age of 16 on, I had always worked Saturday nights, which meant I usually would get to bed sometime between three and four in the morning. For me, a Sunday afternoon nap was always a higher priority than watching football.

Although I am not a fan of football, I do believe the industry has a lot to teach us about running our restaurants and bars. Everyone involved in each football organization has a specific set of jobs to do. I know this probably sound cliché, but when I talk about the football organization, I'm talking about more than just the players and coaches. The success or failure of a football team goes much deeper than just that. And the same is true with your business. The importance of understanding this and acting on it is one of the keys to your businesses' future success.

Think about your favorite football team. Who is involved in making sure the team wins every week? The first thing you probably thought of was the players. The players are like your front of house staff. They are the people who are interacting with your guests. Just as the team has different positions for the players, so does your team. If you're running a restaurant, these people are your hosts, waiters, and bussers.

A footballs team's coaches are like your management staff. You are the head coach; your departments and shift managers are like the offensive and defensive coaches. You've probably figured this much out on your own.

Here's what most people miss – there are so many more jobs within a football organization that are vital to the success of the team; jobs the average fan doesn't even know exist. But they are jobs of critical importance to the team's impressive victory or crushing defeat. There are player scouts, video analysts, medical staff, a director of performance and nutrition, salary cap analyst, strength and conditioning coaches, equipment technicians, and field technicians to name a few. As you can see, beyond the coach and players, there are literally hundreds of people who are involved with each and every football team.

In order for a team to succeed, every single one of the hundreds of people who make up a football organization must know exactly what is expected of them. Each person must also know what to expect from everyone else too.

The same is true with your business. Your employees, every single one of them in every single position from the cleaning staff right on up to yourself, need to know exactly what is expected of them by every other position *and* they need to know what they can expect from everyone else working.

I used to *think* we did this, but I was wrong. I used to thoroughly explain to each and every employee exactly what his or her job duties were. I was really organized and professional with it too. I typed up job responsibilities and had them printed in a bound file for each position, and I would give that to each new hire. Waitresses were responsible for making guests felt welcomed, taking food and drink orders, delivering purchased products, checking on guests and giving guests their check. Cleaning staff was responsible for vacuuming and mopping floors, wiping down counters and glass, cleaning bathrooms, and so on. You get the picture.

As I dug into creating CREST, I realized I was training my staff completely backwards. I have a lot of friends in the hospitality business, so I went around asking them how they train their staff. What I discovered was that every single restaurant owner I talked to train their staff the same (wrong) way I was training my staff. Everyone single one of them was training with job duties.

Employees were so focused on doing their own jobs; they were for the most part oblivious to what other staff member's needs were. This disconnect between staff members resulted in a disconnect with our guests. The final product we were trying to produce was exceptional experiences that make our guests happy, but employees were task focused, not customer focused. **They were delivering the product, but not the experience.**

Creating incredible guest experiences is where the real money is at. When you can get your staff to work together to provide guest experiences that keep them coming back and bringing their friends and family with them, the door to massive profits opens like it's on greased hinges.

Realizing I had to find a way to get my staff to work toward our common purpose of creating happiness, I decided to have separate meetings with each group of employees. I met separately with shift managers, bartenders, wait staff, cooks, party hosts, lane attendants, and janitorial staff. Like me, you probably have some staff members who work in multiple positions. I had them attend each of the meetings which pertained to their positions.

For these meetings, I arranged the tables in a circle so everyone could see everyone else. This is important. You want to create an environment where constructive discussion will take place.

I asked them three questions:

1. What do expect from each of the other employee positions?
2. What do other employee positions expect from you?
3. What do our guests expect from you?

I'll be honest; when I first came up with the idea for these meetings, I was less than excited. I had to have a lot of meetings, and I honestly didn't think I would be able to get everyone onboard with what I was trying to accomplish. I was wrong. Everyone appreciated being able to help form our training. Now, these are my favorite meetings of the entire year. In fact, I do these meetings twice a year. I'll summarize the information and have a second meeting with all of my staff members to go over what everyone in all the different positions discussed. These exercises absolutely transformed my entire staff and my business. Here's how:

First, your staff will start to take ownership in your business. Remember our discussion about company culture? I told you that company culture is not a "thing" that is handed to a person. You cannot have someone read a book or watch a video and instantly understand and buy into your company culture. Your staff needs to be assimilated into your company culture. These discussions on expectations are a huge part of that. They get to help shape how your business functions. And when it essentially comes from your staff through discussion and not directly from you, they become personally invested.

Second, it truly does define how the guest experience is created from the moment your guests walk in the door all the way through to when they drive out of your parking lot. Remember, your job in these meetings is being the moderator and recorder. When someone brings up an issue that they see as a problem, probe that and ask questions about it. Then ask your staff for solutions. Not only will they solve problems that you didn't even know existed, but you'll also find new and better ways to improve the consistency and efficiency of your processes. Your staff members are smart and good at what they do. Let them help shape how your business functions.

And finally, you'll get a unique insight into what your customers want and expect. Businesses spend a ton of time and money doing research trying to figure out what people want. I read a lot of articles that talk about the consumer research that's being done to figure out consumer shopping habits. Call me old-fashioned, but I believe the fastest and easiest way to figure out what people want is to listen to them.

Nowadays, everyone has an opinion about just about everything, and they're not afraid to let everyone know. One simple way to make your customer happy is to give them what they want. The problem is that most of the time, people won't give you their honest opinion. Sure, there's always that one guy who's more than happy to let you know how much he hates the type of pickles you serve or that the color on your walls sucks (my 5-year-old, Luke, is like that guy – absolutely no filter!). But most people don't want to tell the owner or manager what's actually going on in their head. Maybe they're afraid they'll get someone in trouble, or maybe they don't think their idea is worth your time. Do you know who they do tell? I guarantee your staff gets an earful both while they're working and even when they're off the clock. Ask your staff. It's a quick, easy, and very reliable way to find out what your customer's expectations are.

Give your guests what they want, when they want, and how they want it will keep them coming back again and again. Meeting and exceeding your customer's expectations is the quick way to board the money train. But wait, it get's better! Wouldn't it be great if you could raise your prices without getting any pushback from your customers? Exceeding your guest's expectations is the key to working less and making more than you ever have before. Do you remember when I talked about succeeding by sucking a little less than your competition? When you properly train your staff to work together to create incredible experiences your customers really desire, you no longer need to compete on price.

When you try to become the lowest priced option, you start playing a game you will eventually loose. Why? Because everyone else can play that same game. It takes no skill or effort to become the lowest priced option. Have you been in the bars that sell the cheapest beer in your town? Is that really what you want to be? Of course not! Over time, all of the "lowest priced" businesses end up going out of business. It's a model that just isn't sustainable.

Before you invest in remodeling your building or purchasing new equipment, you need to invest in your staff. Dollar for dollar, your return on investment will be way above anything else you can do in your business.

I'm going to let you in on a secret that has made me a lot of money: virtually none of your competition is willing to put in the time and effort to a training program for their staff that will create the unforgettable guest experiences you've just learned about. It takes time to find all the pieces, sit down with your staff, create your company culture, and mold them into lean, mean, money-making machines. Be more than just a bar or restaurant. Make your business a destination, and you'll no longer have competition, you'll become the five star competition everyone else measures themselves against.

Chapter 7
CREATING CREDIBILITY

I love living in northern Wisconsin. It is a great place to raise a family. And being the father of eight kids, that works out pretty well for me. I especially love the outdoors. I can literally drive for less than an hour in any direction and find some incredible wonder of nature that my family can enjoy for the day.

As much as I love Wisconsin, I find it exciting traveling to distant destinations throughout the United States visiting all of the incredible small towns in our great nation. One of my favorite parts of visiting someplace new is checking out the locally run establishments. From shopping to dining to eating, I truly enjoy getting a taste of the local fare and engaging in wonderful conversation with some of the most interesting people I've ever met.

What drives me nuts is traveling with friends who only want to go to the same restaurants they have back home. I keep telling them that the McDonalds in Nashville is exactly the same as the McDonalds in Merrill, Wisconsin. The last thing I want to do when I'm visiting a new place is to go to an Applebee's or Red Robin. It's not that I don't like the food at those restaurants. Like I said before, I love to get a real taste of the local flavor by going to the corner BBQ shop or the mom and pop diner down the street.

So why is it you'll find a McDonalds in every single city in America and in just about every major city throughout the entire world? Why is it that these chains and franchises are always so busy, especially with out of town traffic? People know exactly what kind of experience they're going to have when they go there, regardless of what city or even what country they are in. And in many cases, it's not even the quality of the food that creates loyalty. It's the consistency of the guest's experience.

Consistent experiences creates credibility with your guests

Working in the hospitality industry, I spend a lot of time with many different people in a social setting. I'm not a fan of small talk, but I've learned to fake it pretty well. I like to sneak out with my wife and friends once in a while to places where people don't know me, so I can enjoy the company I'm with. There is one particular trendy restaurant we used go to once in a while. They prepare dishes with all locally sourced ingredients. They have spent a lot of money fixing up an old warehouse giving the place a really fun, trendy vibe. The first time we went there, everything was fantastic. A friendly hostess greeted us at the door, the bartender was very knowledgeable and efficient, our waitress was great, and the food looked delicious and tasted even better. The service was outstanding. Even the bussers had a smile on their faces and thanked us for stopping in. All in all, we had a great experience.

Having eight kids in the house makes it a little difficult to get out, but about a month later the planets aligned again, so I called the same restaurant and made a reservation. We were all looking forward to our night out. My wife and I got dressed up, I rented a movie on Amazon for the kids, popped lots of popcorn, gave detailed babysitting instructions to my older boys, and headed out the door. The minute I met our waitress, I knew our night out was in trouble.

Her name was Vikki. She was nice enough, but you could tell she thought she had better things to do than take care of us. After being seated, it took us no less than 20 minutes to get our drinks. I glanced over at the bar and noticed it wasn't too busy, but the bartender seemed to be struggling to keep up. The worst part was I could see him get in constant verbal arguments with the wait staff. On the upside, we had a lot of time to decide what we wanted to order since we had to wait so long for our drinks, but finding Vikki was all but impossible. I was able to wave a busser over to our table and asked them to find Vikki for us. He seemed surprised that a guest actually talked to him. Thankfully, he found Vikki, and she took our order.

The rest of the evening continued down that same road of disappointment. The food was pretty good, but the service was lousy. Two visits, two very different experiences. I have visited that restaurant two more times since that fateful day. Once the experience was pretty average, and the other time the food was way off. I might give them one more chance, but my time out is valuable to me, and I'm not much of a gambler. I don't want to have to check the over/under before we go out to see what my chances of having a good experience are going to be. Because of their lack of consistency, that restaurant has absolutely no credibility.

That restaurant obviously did not have a system in place to consistently create great guests experiences. My time, just like yours is valuable and in high demand. I don't want to waste my time going to a restaurant where I've got a 50/50 chance of enjoying myself. You need to implement CREST in your business to give your customers a solid guarantee they'll have a great visit. Otherwise, they'll be gone like a puff of smoke and you may never see them again.

Giving your guests consistent experiences is key to creating strong, continual growth in your business. After I bought my business from my parents, revenue was growing slowly, but growth stalled out at $750,000. It wasn't until I started focusing my efforts on providing consistently superior experiences for my guests that my business really started to take off. Over the course of just a couple of years, I've grown revenue to over $1,000,000!

When you create systems to continually train your staff to create consistent experiences that bring your guests happiness, you'll not only be earning five star reviews, but your restaurant's revenues will steadily grow for years to come.

Chapter 8

GET IN THE CLONING BUSINESS

Do you remember the inventor, Ron Popeil? I might be giving away my age here, but when I was a kid, Ron Popeil had infomercials for goofy kitchen gadgets on the TV all the time. He sold all different kinds of appliances and kitchen tools that he said made cooking cleaner and easier. One of the items he sold was his Showtime Rotisserie & BBQ. That item went on to sell over 8 million units. One of his big selling points on this particular product was that you could put your favorite kind of meat in this contraption with a bunch of tasty spices, set the timer, and come back hours later to a delicious meal. My absolute favorite part of those infomercials was when he would get the whole crowd to say together "set it and forget it!"

You're probably wondering why I'm brining up infomercials when I'm supposed to be talking about customer service. Let me ask you this – do you think Ron Popeil would have sold 8 million of his Showtime Rotisserie & BBQ if he had to sell each one himself face to face with his customers? Heck no! So how did he do it? He created systems that allowed him to make the sale without doing all the work himself.

Have you ever seen the movie Multiplicity? It's a movie from the 90's where the main character played by Michael Keaton plays an overworked husband and contractor who is having trouble getting everything done so he finds a way to make copies of himself. Things don't work out so well for Keaton and his dopplegangers, but wouldn't it be amazing if there were more of you to get things done?

In your business, nobody is ever going to care about your business more than you do. If you had ten copies of yourself, you could be everywhere in your business doing everything all the time. That way you would be absolutely certain your guests would recieve consistently outstanding experiences that your business needs to provide to make massive profits. Obviously that's impossible, but it *is* possible to create systems to get your employees to do what you want them to do even when you're not physically there.

So what are these systems? In a computer, the operating system is the program that allows you to create documents, write emails, watch videos, or surf the Internet. It's the backbone that gives you the ability to use the programs on your computer. In a similar way, you need to create systems in your business that empower your employees to make you money by creating consistently exceptional experiences for your guests. In a way, this goes all the way back to your company culture. The systems you implement are there to help your employees create happiness for your guests which also continuously instill your company culture.

Chapter 9

RAISE YOUR STANDARDS

So let's go back to our common purpose for a minute, which for my business is to create happiness and lasting friendships for people of all ages. How do we make that happen? This is where we go back to the Disney model of customer service and create our Quality Standards. Your quality standards are the guidelines that you use to achieve your common purpose. They are the measuring stick that you will use to judge how to deal with every situation your employees will have to deal with while working.

It's important to take a step back here and remember that everything we are talking about throughout this entire book applies to every single one of your employees. Every single one of your employees should be trained on this, not just the front of house employees. In fact, if you have third-party vendors doing work inside your business, you should seriously consider training them too. Everyone from the cleaning service you contract to your cooks to your wait staff is all ultimately serving your guests.

What I'm about to tell you, if implemented correctly, will be a game changer for your business. It will direct every decision you make. It will determine who you hire and who you fire. It will be the backbone of every training session you have. You'll use it to praise your staff and to help them grow when they fall short.

In order of importance, here are your QUALITY STANDARDS:

1. SAFETY
2. COURTESY
3. SHOW
4. CONSISTENCY
5. EFFICIENCY

No longer will you have to worry about sucking a little less than the competition. This is how you beat the big guys. This is how you succeed. This is how you create credibility by providing consistent guest experiences. This is how you get your life back.

Disney is the originator of quality standards. When working to become the best, we look to the best for guidance. Let's take a quick look at each quality standard and see what they mean to your business.

Number 1 – SAFETY

Safety is the first on the list because it really is the most important. The safety of your guests and employees must always be paramount. Some examples of safety are:

- Cleaning up a spill on the floor that might be a slipping hazard.
- Shoveling and salting icy entrances.
- Checking guest identification to prevent underage persons from gaining access to alcohol.
- Controlling alcohol service to ensure no one is over-served.
- A properly lit parking lot.

Safety is the first and most important quality standard; it trumps all other quality standards. That doesn't mean the other quality standards can be ignored; it means that you apply safety in lieu of the other standards.

I was out to eat with my wife and kids a couple of weeks back. We were at a fast food restaurant and my five-year-old spilled his soda on the floor. My wife jumped up to clean it up with a bunch of napkins. The spill wasn't that bad, and she could have quickly done it herself, but I wanted to see what their staff's response would be to the situation. So I stopped my wife and walked up to the order counter and told an employee that my child had spilled his soda on the floor. I had cut in line because I knew it was a safety concern. Without a word, the employee immediately stopped taking the order from the customer he was working with, went to the back counter, tossed me a towel, and went back to taking the guests order.

Granted, they weren't using my CREST customer service, but whatever they were teaching their employees didn't work. Here's how my staff would have handled that same situation:

Upon being informed of the spill, the staff member would politely excuse herself for a moment, tell a manager what had happened, and either cleaned up the spill herself while the manager took her position taking orders, or the manager would have cleaned up the spill while the staff member went back to taking orders.

Either way, the guest whose order was being taken would have been politely asked to wait so we could clean up a spill before someone slips and falls. My staff would have also gone the extra mile by refilling the spilled soda.

Throwing a towel at a guest expecting them to clean it up is a safety fail (how well will they actually clean it up?), and it's a courtesy fail (the guest should never be expected to clean up after themselves like that). Taking care of a safety issue right away also shows all of your guests that you honestly care about each and every one of your guests.

Number 2 – COURTESY

Number two on the list is courtesy. It is the second most important standard because we are dealing with people, and people want to be treated with courtesy and respect. But it goes much deeper than just saying please and thank you. You need to teach your staff to show your guests a deep and honest feeling of gratitude. Some examples of courtesy are:

- Acknowledging a guest with a simple "nice to see you."
- If you're too busy to serve someone right away, acknowledge him or her and tell them you'll be with them in a minute.
- Have "customer centric" conversations.
- Use phrases like "my pleasure" instead of "no problem."
- Be proactive looking for problems before guests have to bring them to your attention.

We are all social creatures. Deep down we not only desire, but require personal, social interactions with other human beings. Over the past 30 years, we have been promised time and time again that technology would be the answer to all of society's social problems. It was promised that instant communication would allow both the quality and number of your friendships to grow; it was said that people would be closer than ever before.

I remember when I got my first modem back in 1991. It was a 1200 baud modem that I hooked up to my parents Macintosh Plus. To give you an idea of how fast that was, a typical modern

60 Mbps Internet service is about 50,000 times faster than my old 1200 baud modem. The first day I got my modem I dialed up my friend across town (there was no DSL or cable modems back then – everything went right over your actual phone line). We were able to type back and forth to each other. Then I figured out where to dial to hook up to a hub to connect to a CRAY super computer in California (there was no world wide web, or www, back then either). From there I could chat with anyone around the world. There were a lot fewer people on the Internet back then, but it instantly made the world seem a lot smaller.

Little did I know the enormous negative impact the Internet would have on society. In his book *"The Revenge of Analogue: Real Things and Why They Matter,"* David Sax details how people are beginning to revolt against the digital world we've been coerced to live in. Real, physical things are making a come back in a big way. People are buying vinyl records, pictures are being shot on real film, and physical bookstores are making a comeback.

This is great news for all of us in the hospitality industry. Let's face it, people could get their dinner, beer, and entertainment from anywhere, even delivered to their doorstep. So why do they take all of the effort to visit you? Because people are people! They hunger and thirst for personal interactions with real people who are really there right in front of them. Treat them like crap, and they'll never come back. Treat them indifferently, and they won't care if they come back or not. But treat them with courtesy and sincere gratitude and get ready to hear the cash register ring.

Number 3 – SHOW

This one comes straight from Disney. Show is everything your guests will experience with their physical senses. What they see, hear, and smell are all part of show. At Walt Disney World, they look at everything as a production. The entire park is basically one big stage.

If it When the stage and cast members (that's what Disney employees are called) are set properly, it's called "good show." If, on the other hand, something is out of place, run down, or a cast member is poorly dressed, it is call "bad show."

Some examples of show are:

- Properly dressed employees with good hygiene.
- Updated, clean bathrooms.
- Clean tables and organized chairs.
- How your food looks and tastes.
- Having the appropriate genre and volume for background music.
- Having the appropriate shows on your televisions.
- Keeping your parking lot and exterior clean and up to date.

Disney goes to great lengths to make sure they always have "good show". In fact, they go so far as to paint the railing in the busy areas of the park every single day so there are no chips or scuffs showing. How much attention do your employees give to the show you're putting on for your guests?

Show is third on the list behind safety and courtesy, and it makes sense when you think about it. I've been in some of the coolest bars with some of the worst customer service. The thing I remember most about those places isn't the multi-million-dollar renovations they did; it wasn't the top-notch entertainment (also show) they brought in. It was the indifferent service we received. There's an old saying, "you can put lipstick on a pig, but it's still a pig."

RAISE YOUR STANDARDS

That being said, it's still very important to have good show in your business; just not at the expense of the other quality standards. If you flip it around and have great courtesy and safety with bad show, your guests will be left with the impression that you're running a dump and that honestly does affect the perception your guests have of their experience.

I am constantly praising my staff for good show and correcting them for bad show. When you put it in terms of being "on stage" in front of your guests, employees start to see that they do have control over many different aspects of their guest's experiences. Running a busy restaurant, I have all different ages of guests coming through my door every day. Our goal is to have sporting events on the television at all times. When a game that was broadcast on one of the national networks is over, you never know what is going to be on next. One time, after a college football game finished at about 3 pm on a Saturday afternoon, the next show was one of those crime investigation shows. I happened to look up at the TV, and someone's head was getting cut off on the show. We had families both on the lanes and in our restaurant at the time! I quickly changed the channel to a sporting event, but that was definitely bad show.

You might be thinking that you keep your business clean and looking good, but that's only half the battle. The way your staff presents themselves, the way they interact with each other, the language they use in the kitchen that can be overheard by guests are all part of show. Sometimes it helps to have someone else come into your business to give you a fresh perspective. I have my business mystery shopped once a month. Getting a narrative from someone else has really helped us address issues that we were completely blind to. Put on a good show along with courtesy and safety, and you'll be well on your way to creating experiences that will bring your guests back again and again.

Numbers 4 & 5 – CONSISTENCY and EFFICIENCY

The last two quality standards on our list are consistency and efficiency. These two are pretty straight forward, and in spite of the fact they are at the bottom of our list of quality standards, they must not be ignored. In fact, if just one of the five quality standards is ignored, your customer service will fail.

Some examples of consistency are:

- Every guest is given the same attention and respect (no playing favorites).
- Food portions are always the same.
- Drinks are prepared the same by all bartenders.
- Interactions with guests are planned and loosely scripted.

RAISE YOUR STANDARDS

Your guest's experience from driving into your parking lot to walking out the door at the end of their visit should be consistent with every other time they visit. That doesn't mean their experiences should be exactly the same. Like we said earlier unless they are at a haunted house, people don't like surprises. People find comfort in consistency.

Some examples of efficiency are:

- Promptly welcoming guests.
- Quickly correcting any problems that may arise.
- Preparing food and drinks with the appropriate speed.
- Cleaning customer areas quickly so next guests can be served.

Efficiency is fairly obvious, but it is absolutely necessary. There is no way I can tell you how long it should take to make a martini, or get a tenderloin steak. Every business is different, but consistent efficiency is important. Unless you're a fast food restaurant, you do not need to get your food order out in less than five minutes. But if you are a fast casual, it shouldn't take 20 minutes for your guests to get their order.

Efficiency isn't just for fast food restaurants. All restaurants need to make efficiency part of their company culture. People's attention spans are much shorter today than they were a few years ago. Just the other day I had a school group in my bowling center and a nine-year-old girl asked me what she should do in between turns. Really? There were about 70 seconds between turns, and she had no idea what to do with herself! You may not have any nine-year-olds coming into your business right now, but she's one of your future customers, and that's the attention span you have to look forward to.

Have you noticed that newspaper and magazine articles have gotten shorter? Attention spans are about 140 characters long. Training your staff to interact with your guests at the appropriate times promptly will be critical to the success of your business in the near future. Integrating systemized efficiency into your business now will put you another step ahead of your competition.

I want to take a minute to emphasize how important it is to integrate all five quality standards into your company culture. Falling short on just one of the quality standards will completely undermine your guest's experience. Consistency creates credibility. If you can't deliver on all five quality standards every time, your customer counts will slowly erode, employees will stop trying to create experiences for your guests that bring them happiness, and your cash flow will dry up.

The amazing thing that happens when you do deliver every experience with safety, courtesy, show, consistency, and efficiency is that your guests will start to identify with your business personally. You'll become their go-to place. When you become exceptionally good at it, price starts to become a non-factor, and you can start to charge what you should be charging. And when people identify as being "part" of your business, they become living, breathing commercials for you. They wear your shirts and sing your praises to everyone they know. That's not only the most effective kind of advertising, it also free!

Chapter 10

AVOIDING HOSTAGE SITUATIONS

I've always hated turnover. Not the pastries – I love those. I'm talking about losing staff. Just when you find the perfect mix of employees, something happens, and a bunch of them quit. And if your business is like mine, you've got TONS of part-time help. Not only is the majority of my staff part-time, most of them are quite young ranging in age from 14 to 30. That's a double whammy.

Here's the problem with hiring part-time help: it takes just as much time and effort to train a part-time employee as it does to train a full-time employee. The difference is you need to train at least two part-time employees to equal one full-time employee. That's double the time, money, and effort.

Have you ever had an employee who had such a negative attitude that they brought everyone around them down? I look at those kinds of employees as if they were a virus. If you don't do whatever it takes to get rid of that disease, it will infect your entire staff. But I didn't always look at it this way. I used to hate training new employees so I would do whatever it took to keep old staff on so I wouldn't have to train in someone new. All that did was make my problem way worse; their bad attitudes infected everyone around them. Then I had huge problems on my hands.

One of the most liberating feelings in business is realizing you aren't dependent upon any one staff member for your businesses success. I'm not saying you don't need employees. What I'm saying is that *everyone* on your staff is replaceable. And I mean everyone. We all think we have that one person who, if they leave, would sink our business. If that's how you're running your business, you are opening yourself up to a kidnapping. Eventually, that person will hold your business for ransom, and you'll give them whatever they want. After all, you couldn't possibly run your business without them, right?

In order to get yourself in a position where everyone is truly replaceable, you must have a system in place to train their replacement. And to be massively successful, you must train your employees how to create memorable experiences for your customers every time they visit. To be perfectly honest, training the particular skill attached to each individual job position isn't really that difficult. If you hire the right people, they will pick up on that stuff fairly quickly. It's the customer service training that takes time and diligence.

You need to create customer service training systems that will quickly and methodically educate your new hires. It needs to be a system that will get them to buy into your new company culture. And it needs to be a system that anyone can implement so you won't need to do all the work yourself.

Implement CREST in your business. Train your staff how to create outstanding customer experiences. Teach them that customer happiness is their ultimate goal. When you do this, you will no longer look at new hires as a training drain on your time. You'll see them as an opportunity to take your business to the next level.

Chapter 11

CONSISTENCY IS KING

Remember how I said creating consistency for your guests makes your business credible? That same equation holds true for the training of your employees. Consistency = Credibility.

If you don't consistently preach and teach your Common Purpose and your Quality Standards, nobody (including yourself) will remember what they are much less use them to create incredible guest experiences that will keep people coming back, again and again, making you more money than you could ever imagine. It just won't happen. You need to preach and teach these ideas ALL THE TIME consistently.

Consistently teach, preach, and model both your Common Purpose and your Quality Standards, and I guarantee your staff will start to pay attention. Like anything new, your staff will get excited about it for a couple of weeks. They'll talk about different situations and how they used their quality standards to create really great guest experiences. If you leave it there and don't retrain and reemphasize the importance and implications of your quality standards, you will have not only wasted a ton of time on your initial training; you'll be walking away from a mountain of future sales.

I've never been a big car guy, but ever since I was nine years old, I've desperately wanted a Shelby Cobra. That Mustang has the perfect mix of sexy curves and crazy power. If I ever win the lottery, that will be my guilty pleasure purchase. What would happen if I decided I wasn't going to take care of that car? No more changing the air filter. No more checking the tire pressure. No more oil changes. No more waxing twice a year. Who in their right mind would spend the money to get a car like that and then not do a thing to take care of it to keep it in top-notch shape? That would be crazy!

Your staff is basically a Shelby Cobra. Labor is one of your biggest expenses - you need to get your staff performing at the highest level possible. And to do that you need to regularly invest time training and coaching them properly.

Investing your time creating an incredible customer service training program like CREST is great, but if you're not willing to continually and systematically continue to train your staff, this new money-making machine will come to a grinding halt. Business, as usual, isn't good enough anymore. In order to consistently earn five star reviews, beat out all of your local competition and compete with the big chains and franchises, continual training is a vital necessity. Turning your staff into customer service superstars is almost like building a money printing machine. But if you neglect the machine, it's going to break down, and you won't be able to print money on demand anymore. Your golden goose will die.

Consistently teach, preach, and model your quality standards and your staff will believe in what you are doing. They will believe that they can create happiness for your guests. They will understand that everyone on your staff is working toward the same goal. The vision you have for your business will become credible and obtainable. And when your ideas start to earn the respect of your staff, you'll start to earn a whole lot more money.

Chapter 12

EXCEPTIONAL PRODUCTIVITY

What are you worth? Before you start adding numbers in your head, I'm not talking about your net worth. Although I'm pretty sure there were times my mother wanted to give me away for free, I vividly remember hearing my mom tell me many times, "Mark, you're worth more than all the money in the world." I'm sure your mother said the same thing, but I'm not talking about how much your mother loves you either. I'm talking about the value of your time and knowledge.

You didn't get to where you are now without learning a thing or two along the way. All the knowledge, experience and expertise that is crammed between your ears is worth so much more than you'll ever give yourself credit for. You need to put all that knowledge to work for you by freeing yourself from day to day operation of your business.

It's going to take a real shift in how you look at your business. What I'm about to tell you has allowed me to grow my business over 33% in less than 24 months. It has allowed me to be the husband, father, and friend I never was before because I was too busy working. It has given me the financial freedom to both reinvest in my business and enjoy my life with my family and friends. These eight words will change your life:

Work on your business, not in your business.

I used to be a great bartender. Not only did I work countless hours slinging drinks, I took pride in my extensive knowledge of exotic cocktails. I've always enjoyed bartending, but there are only so many hours in a day, and my wife made it abundantly clear that if I took any more time away from our family, I'd be living in a box in the front yard paying child support for eight kids. I knew I had to work on growing my business if I was going to realize my financial goals, but I also needed to be working in my business to fill shifts and make sure everything would run smoothly. I felt like I was stuck between a rock and a hard place.

This was right about this time that I discovered the writings of a guy named Dan Kennedy. His most significant contribution to the business community has been in implementing direct response marketing. But he also preaches personal productivity. He's the guy who told me to work on my business, not just in my business.

That got me thinking – a lot. I started looking at all the small jobs I was doing around my business. I quickly realized I was constantly wasting my valuable time doing jobs I could pay someone minimum wage to do. On top of that, I was working some of the least profitable shifts. I never wanted to hire in staff when we were slow, so I worked those shifts myself. My thought was why pay someone to work when we're not making much money. I could just work the shift myself. After all, I was paying myself salary so it didn't cost me anything to work a few more hours.

I decided to make a change and work on growing my business through staff training, creating marketing campaigns, and most importantly reading and educating myself. When I started investing my time into working *on* my business, I started making a whole lot more money. In fact, I joke with people that the more time I spend in my office, the more money I make. I'm still in my business when we're open, but I've changed the reason why I'm there. Instead of being just an employee, I've made myself the face of my restaurant, bar, and bowling alley.

There are some drawbacks to taking this approach. I am now my own worst bartender, but being in my business when we're open without working in my business has allowed me to create friendships and connections with my guests. It gives them an intimate connection to me and my business that makes them feel like they are part of my business.

It makes me cry inside a little when I think about how much money I lost out on over the years. If I could only go back ten years, implement CREST back then and do it all over again…

Once you properly delegate tasks within your business freeing your time up so you can work on your business instead of just in your business, one of your top priorities must be the continual training your staff. Implementing the systems and strategies you've learned in this book will create an immediate energy within your staff. It's like lighting a fireplace. When you first get the fire going, it's super hot. But if you don't tend to the fire, it quickly dies down. And if you completely ignore it, it will go out completely and relighting the fire becomes very difficult. You need to keep that fire going by continually tending to it, adding more wood, and stoking it.

The same is true with firing up your staff. When you first implement your new customer service system, your employees are going to be really excited to create amazing experiences for your guests, and I guarantee you'll have immediate success. The problem is the fire, excitement, and commitment of your staff will quickly die off, just as an untended fire will. You need to stoke the fire and add fuel to the fire on a regular basis. That's what continual training is for.

When dealing with part-time staff, continual training and reinforcement is vitally important. With full-time staff, their job is a huge part of their lives, but with part-time staff, it's just a blip on their radar. You need to continually and constantly reinforce the concepts and procedures you put in place. If you don't, the fire goes out, and you're right back where you started. Actually, you'll be in an even worse position. Your guests will have experienced exceptional service and will quickly come to expect it. If you don't put a system in place to keep your staff on track, the whole train will derail, and you'll lose all of those new and profitable customers.

You are talented and gifted. Use the people around you properly so you'll have the time and energy to apply your talents to your business on a consistent, regular basis and you'll start to see how much your time is actually worth. And I guarantee you it's a lot more than what you might think it is.

Chapter 13

MISSED MEMORIES, NEW OPPORTUNITIES

Owning and managing a business is a hard life. Most people don't get this. Just about everything else in your life takes a back seat to your business. It's not fair! Other people get to punch a clock and go home. Their work doesn't come right on home with them. But for you and me it's a different story.

I can't tell you how many times I've had to leave dinner early, miss my kids opening their birthday presents, cut short a night out with friends, or cancel a date with my wife. Just because we manage or own a business shouldn't mean we can't have a life outside and separate from work. But the massive success or imminent failure of your business is dependent upon your guests giving you their money. And that won't happen over and over again if they're not happy.

But is it really worth missing out on all of those wonderful, memorable life moments? No amount of money can buy you back one millisecond of time. You can't search eBay to buy back those missed moments. No amount of success or fame will ever make up for missing even just one of those precious moments.

I have a very good friend who is a network engineer. He was living very comfortably making six figures with eight weeks of vacation annually. About a year ago, we met up for beers, and he tells me he's quitting his job and going back to school to become a radiologist. I knew he hated his job, but damn. It takes balls to walk away from a job like that. So why did he do it? Because his job was making him absolutely miserable. No amount of money was worth the constant pile of crap they were heaping on him day after day.

We should work to live, not live to work.

Like I said before, I have a lot of young people who work for me. I know that for most, their job with me is just a stepping-stone to bigger things. Many of them tell me about their dreams and aspirations, which almost always revolve around the career they, want to pursue. I find it sad that we often define ourselves by what we do for a living. We should be defining ourselves by the lives we live outside of work.

Unfortunately for you and me, it's not always that simple. The responsibilities that are heaped upon your shoulders can seem crushing at times and the headaches of managing so many part-time and full-time staff members follow you wherever you go. If you're going to run a truly successful restaurant, you need to create a steady stream of happy customers. But don't do it at the expense of living your own life on your own terms.

The systems that make up CREST will absolutely set you free. Sure you'll start making more money. But more importantly you'll be able to leave your business worry free knowing that your team is running on a system; a system that provides you with a healthy, consistent stream of revenue. They'll become a machine that, if properly maintained, will make you massive profits whether you're there or not.

Chapter 14

EXCEPTIONAL SUCCESS

What was the last investment you made in your business? It seems there's always something needed – a new freezer, updated website, or new furniture. Although all of these things are necessary, they will never give you the return on investment you'll get when you invest in your staff.

Investing in your staff, transforming them into customer service legends will not only earn you five star reviews and make your restaurant and bar the talk of the town, it will make you a whole lot more money.

Think about it – your freezer doesn't convince your customers to hand over money. When was the last time your furniture made a sale? The one thing that makes the biggest impact on not only how much money you make from your guests per visit, but also how often they come in, is your staff. There is no newspaper, radio, television, or Internet ad in the world that can have even a fraction of the impact a properly trained staff will have on your guests. And the best part is NONE OF YOUR COMPETITION IS DOING THIS!

Are you ready to turn your staff into customer service superstars so they can create extraordinary experiences for your guests getting them to come back time and again spending more money than ever before? The famous Chinese philosopher Lao Tzu once said, "the journey of one thousand miles begins with a single step." In your case, the journey leads to a big pile of cash, but the journey doesn't need to take all that long.

Do you want to instantly transform your staff into the customer service legends and money making machines you need to grow your business without having to create all of the systems, templates, scripts, and processes yourself? I've packaged all of this valuable information into an easy to implement training system called **The Money Making Customer Service Blueprint**.

This powerful staff training system is based on the CREST customer service system outlined in the book and includes even more detailed training modules for training both your managers and your general staff along with monthly training sessions to help you train them on a consistent, continual basis to keep that customer service fire stoked. Simply go to **HappyCustomerFormula.com/bestintown** right now to take the first step to creating massive profits.

The late great W. Edwards Deming once said, "If you can't describe what you are doing as a process, you don't know what you're doing."

Success isn't an accident; it happens when daring individuals take bold action. To discover even more about Becoming the Best In Town and Creating Customer Service Legends and Massive Profits, go to www.HappyCustomerFormula.com/bestintown to get

access to The Money Making Customer Service Blueprint staff training system and start creating consistently exceptional guests experiences.

www.ingramcontent.com/pod-product-compliance
Lightning Source LLC
Chambersburg PA
CBHW070209230526
45471CB00002B/885